The
LITTLE BOOK OF
VEGAN
STUDENT FOOD

T0349804

THE LITTLE BOOK OF VEGAN STUDENT FOOD

An Hachette UK Company
www.hachette.co.uk

Summersdale Publishers
Part of Octopus Publishing Group Limited
Carmelite House
50 Victoria Embankment
LONDON
EC4Y 0DZ
UK

www.summersdale.com

Printed and bound in Poland

ISBN: 978-1-83799-276-8

Substantial discounts on bulk quantities of Summersdale books are available to corporations, professional associations and other organizations. For details contact general enquiries: telephone: +44 (0) 1243 771107 or email: enquiries@summersdale.com.

Disclaimer
Neither the author nor the publisher can be held responsible for any injury, loss or claim - be it health, financial or otherwise - arising out of the use, or misuse, of the suggestions made herein. Always consult your doctor before trying any new diet if you have a medical or health condition, or are worried about any of the side effects. This book is not intended as a substitute for the medical advice of a doctor or physician.

The
LITTLE BOOK OF
VEGAN
STUDENT FOOD

Jai Breitnauer

Contents

Introduction

University is a time of adventure, and there is no greater adventure than learning how to cook. Lifelong friendships are cemented over dinner, and shared culinary experience is a valuable form of communal exploration. Whether you are just embarking on your university or college journey or are returning for another, perhaps your final, year, knowing how to whip up an affordable, delicious and impressive meal is a skill that will carry you through your studies and indeed, through life.

There are approximately 88 million vegans around the world today, with approximately 50 per cent of students saying they eat plant-based food most or all of the time. Done right, a vegan diet is packed full of brain-boosting nutrients, is low in cholesterol and is high in complex carbs and protein. It packs a real health punch, helping to ward off seasonal bugs and keep your mind sharp. In addition, studies have shown repurposing grazing land to grow crops could remove 8.1 billion metric tonnes of carbon from the atmosphere every year. A climate-positive future is within the grasp of your vegan hands.

A vegan diet can be lighter on the wallet too. One of the biggest concerns young vegan students often have is the price of food. Others are worried their cooking skills aren't up to par, or that they need expensive, special equipment.

Don't panic! The good news is that with a little help you can be a vegan cookery pro. Vegan food doesn't have to be pricey or complicated. This book will talk you through some simple tricks, tips and recipes that will have you producing mouth-watering, green cuisine that doesn't break the bank, in no time.

We'll cover everything: from quick meals, brain-boosting snacks and drinks, to batch cooking, comfort food and how to impress your friends whether they're vegan or not. And the really good news? You'll never need to learn how to boil an egg.

THE BASICS

Take a deep breath and remember: cooking is about having fun. Stuff will burn. You will get the consistency wrong. You will guestimate the sugar and find the result too sweet, or you will add some extra spices and find the outcome too strong. It doesn't matter.

As long as you have a good grasp of the basics, no disaster will be unrecoverable. This chapter will show you how to stay safe, how to stay healthy, talk you through the equipment you will need and how to measure ingredients. It will help you understand common cooking terms, know where to find those essential nutrients and give you a basic shopping list from which most meals can be built.

What You Need

All you need to start your cooking adventure is a bit of time – set aside 30–60 minutes – some basic equipment, a few easy-to-find ingredients and this handy little book. Don't worry if your kitchen is not palatial. If you're living in catered halls of residence you may only have a kitchenette. That's okay, many of the recipes in this book can be made on a hob. Some might require an oven or grill.

Make sure you have at least one big frying pan and one big saucepan, plus a wooden spoon, a mixing bowl and a baking tray. Most measurements are in cups and spoons so scales aren't necessary, and there is a conversion chart on pages 12–13. If you can afford a good set of cup and spoon measures, that's great. If not, a standard mug filled three-quarters of the way is approximately one 250-ml cup of liquid, while a level-ish spoon is approximately the same as an official measure.

Health and Safety

This isn't a phrase often associated with student kitchens, but you want to be producing food, not *E. coli*. Follow these simple rules to keep the kitchen safe to use:

- **Have a weekly cleaning rota. Wipe surfaces before preparing food.**

- **Many perishable items will have a use-by date, after which food can't be consumed. If they have a best-before date and you've passed it, a quick sniff will usually confirm edibility. A sour smell usually means it's past it. Check the fridge weekly and chuck out anything that's off.**

- **If you've cooked a meal, you can store leftovers in the fridge for up to two days, or in the freezer for three months. Write the date it was cooked on the lid.**

- **Defrost everything thoroughly overnight in the fridge and don't refreeze or reheat more than once.**

- **Empty the bin!**

Conversions and Measurements

Most of the recipes use cups and spoon measurements, but some will use grams. If you prefer using imperial (and you don't have a smartphone to do the conversions for you), here are some basic tables:

25 g ≈ 1 oz	15 ml ≈ ½ fl oz
60 g ≈ 2 oz	30 ml ≈ 1 fl oz
85 g ≈ 3 oz	75 ml ≈ 2½ fl oz
115 g ≈ 4 oz	120 ml ≈ 4 fl oz
255 g ≈ 9 oz	270 ml ≈ 9 fl oz

All spoon measures refer to level spoons, not heaped. Spoon measures can also be substituted for grams with certain ingredients, which is handy for those without a set of kitchen scales.

Obviously, the weights of all ingredients will vary, but here are some rough measures:

1 tbsp ≈ 25 g (1 oz)
2 tbsp ≈ 60 g (2 oz)
3 tbsp ≈ 85 g (3 oz)
4 tbsp ≈ 115 g (4 oz)

Where given in this book, oven temperatures are in Celsius, Fahrenheit and gas mark, but as a rule of thumb for cooking purposes Celsius is roughly half the Fahrenheit temperature. Set fan-assisted ovens 20°C (approximately 70°F) lower and reduce the time spent cooking by 10 minutes for every hour of cooking time.

Glossary of Cooking Terms

Bake – To dry cook food in the oven at a lower temperature for longer.

Baste – To add moisture to food while cooking to stop it drying out.

Beat – To rapidly mix two or more ingredients together with a fork or whisk.

Blanch – To dip vegetables in boiling water for a short period, often around 30 seconds–1 minute, then put them immediately into cold water.

Blend – To mix two or more ingredients together by hand with a spoon or spatula.

Boil – To cook food in water that has reached 100°C (200°F).

Braise – To brown food in a pan first, then finish cooking by simmering in a small amount of liquid.

Brown – To cook over a high heat to brown and/or crisp up the outside of food.

Caramelize – To either cook sugar over a low heat to turn it into a liquid, or to cook a vegetable slowly to release the natural sugars.

Deseed – To open a fruit and remove the seeds inside before cooking.

Dice – To cut into small cubes about 1 cm by 1 cm.

Garnish – To decorate food with something edible.

Grease – To rub a pan with oil to prevent food sticking when cooking.

Julienne – To cut vegetables into matchsticks for stir frying or to garnish.

Knead – To stretch, roll and fold dough before baking.

Marinate – To soak food in a seasoned liquid before cooking, usually overnight.

Mince – To chop something very, very small.

Purée – To cook and then blend, mash and/or strain food. Passata is cooked and strained tomatoes.

Roast – To cook food in the oven at a higher temperature. Usually requires additional oil.

Roux – A mixture of flour and fat used to thicken sauces.

Scant – A measure of ingredients slightly below the lip of the measuring cup.

Skin – To remove the skin on the outside of a fruit or vegetable.

Simmer – To reduce boiling fluids down to a light bubble.

Healthy Vegan Eating

It's easy to fall into unhealthy eating habits when you're living away from home. Relying on convenience food isn't just expensive, your health can pay the price too.

In her book *Unprocessed*, author and psychologist Kimberley Wilson argues poor nutrition from processed foods is contributing to societal mental-health problems and even lowering IQ averages across populations. Processed foods also contain higher levels of sugar, salt and fat, contributing to heart problems and obesity.

Understanding the food groups can help you to properly fuel your brain and body.

PROTEIN

Protein contains amino acids, the building blocks of our bodies that help repair muscles and bones plus make hormones and enzymes. Protein also maintains energy and concentration.

It's a myth that vegan diets don't contain enough protein. Good sources of protein include soy, tofu, lentils and beans, plus oats and grains like quinoa. Seitan, which this book will teach you to make (see page 54), is an affordable and protein-rich meat alternative.

CARBOHYDRATES

The most important thing to understand about carbohydrates is that they aren't all the same. The carbs you want in your diet are long-chain, like brown rice and root vegetables – they break down slowly, introducing glucose into your body in a moderate way to sustain your activities. Short-chain carbohydrates like white bread and pasta flood your system with sugars, creating an energy spike and then a crash, causing tiredness and a tendency to snack.

FATS

Many of us have been raised to believe fat is bad, but the truth is everyone needs a daily dose of healthy fats to function. Dietary fats protect your organs and help digest other essential nutrients. They can even lower cholesterol and help prevent heart disease.

Eat unsaturated fats found in vegetable oils, nuts, seeds and avocados, and avoid saturated and trans fats.

Saturated fats mostly come from animal products, so you're already ahead of the game, and trans fats mostly occur in highly processed foods.

VITAMINS AND MINERALS

Kimberley Wilson makes it very clear in her book that vegans should take supplements, and most dieticians agree. Omega-3s, vitamins B12 and D are essential to support healthy function in vegans. The rest of your vitamin needs can be met by eating wholefoods.

The only tip you really need is eat the rainbow. If your plate is looking beige, it likely won't contain what you need in it. (Natural) colours are king.

Western diets in particular are also lacking in iodine, calcium and zinc. Tofu, almonds and broccoli are a good source of calcium while sea vegetables, like nori, contain iodine. Chickpeas, nuts and pumpkin seeds contain lots of zinc and, again, a good daily supplement will help bolster natural intake.

WATER

When you're studying hard, enjoying nights out with friends, and rushing around trying not to be late for lectures, it's easy to get dehydrated. The average human should be drinking around 3 litres of fluids a day. The good news is that tea and coffee, fruit juice and plant milk count, but water is best. Being well-hydrated keeps you alert and maintains joint and kidney health. Keep a bottle with you and refill it during the day.

The Store Cupboard

The secret of any successful chef is having the additional elements of a good recipe ready to go in your store cupboard, such as stock, oil and dried pasta or rice, so you don't have to think too hard about planning.

BROWN RICE

A versatile, healthy staple that can form the basis of a variety of meals.

CANNED TOMATOES

Canned tomatoes are inexpensive, versatile and easy to use in many recipes.

LEMON JUICE

A splash of lemon can really make the difference to a variety of recipes. Bottled juice is affordable and can be kept in the fridge for long periods.

LINSEED

Also known as flaxseed, linseed is a great binder or egg substitute.

MIXED NUTS

Chopped mixed nuts are great as a topping for salads, soups and curries. They also work well in baking.

NUTRITIONAL YEAST

This inactivated yeast will add zing to creamy or cheesy dishes, and it is also a source of B12.

OIL

Keep a small bottle for salad dressings, but for cooking use canola (rapeseed) oil. Canola oil is an affordable, unsaturated fat that's perfect for frying.

PASTA

Pasta is helpful to keep in the cupboard because it's fast-cooking and versatile.

STOCK POWDER

Almost all recipes either require or can be improved by using a good vegetable stock base.

Spices, Herbs and Seasonings

Important in all cooking, the addition of flavours beyond the basic ingredients is even more essential in vegan cuisine. For example, with some well-placed smoked paprika, garlic, salt and white wine vinegar, you can transform a carrot into smoked "salmon". Without the extras, a carrot is just a carrot!

If you've got a sunny window ledge then you could save yourself some money and brighten up your room by growing basil, parsley, coriander and thyme in a mini fresh herb garden – perfect for garnishing food and adding a bit of flourish. But a good supply of dried herbs and spices in the cupboard will mean you can turn almost anything into a delicious meal without additional shopping or planning ahead.

SALT AND PEPPER

Invest in a good set of grinders, if possible, as rock salt and freshly ground black pepper can transform a meal –

but also have a stash of fine salt for cooking. Top tip: Buy iodized salt to improve your dietary iodine intake.

DRIED MIXED HERBS

Many recipes call for fresh herbs. Unless they're to be used as a garnish, these can often be substituted with dried mixed herbs.

DRIED SPICES

The essential dried spices to keep in stock are:

- **Chilli flakes**
- **Cinnamon**
- **Coriander**
- **Cumin**
- **Garam masala**
- **Garlic powder**
- **Ginger**
- **Onion powder**
- **Paprika**
- **Turmeric**

FRESH FLAVOURS

Add a garlic bulb and a small nobble of ginger to your weekly shopping list – you won't regret it! Fresh chillies are good too. The flavour profile of these fresh items is different to dried and the two can't always be easily exchanged.

FAST AND FLAVOURSOME

One of the things you will probably discover quickly as a student is that you are always in a rush. This isn't necessarily because of poor planning, but because there is always something interesting going on, lots of things to do and somewhere else to be! Having a repertoire of quick meals you can produce will keep you fuelled, save you some money and help you get the most out of student life. Some of the recipes in this chapter create more than one serving, so you can prepare multiple meals that'll require even less prep time.

If you have a good store cupboard (see pages 20–21), then chances are you will always be able to make a meal. The recipes in this chapter are fast – taking under 30 minutes to make – and need just a few ingredients. Most importantly, they're still bang full of flavour.

Mexican Bowl in Minutes

This super-quick, protein-rich Mexican meal works for breakfast, lunch or dinner.

Serves 4

INGREDIENTS

2 cups brown rice
200-g can sweetcorn
1 tbsp oil
400-g can black beans
Dash of Tabasco sauce
Pinch of salt
2 tomatoes, chopped
½ red onion, chopped
2 cloves garlic, crushed
1 tsp paprika
1 tbsp lemon juice
1 avocado
1 pot vegan yoghurt
Handful of coriander (optional)

METHOD

Put the rice on to boil. Open the can of sweetcorn and drain it. Open the can of black beans, drain, rinse and place them in a pan with the oil. Fry on a very low heat with a dash of Tabasco and a pinch of salt.

Combine the tomatoes, red onion, garlic, paprika and lemon juice in a bowl. In a separate bowl, mash the avocado with the back of a fork.

Place a serving of rice in a bowl and top with a spoonful each of the sweetcorn, black beans, tomatoes, avocado and yoghurt. Garnish with the coriander.

Coronation Coins

Coronation Chicken was created to celebrate Queen Elizabeth II's coronation in 1953. This easy version uses a chickpea filling in pastry "coins".

Serves 2–4

INGREDIENTS

400-g can chickpeas
¼ cup mango chutney
¼ cup vegan yoghurt
2 tbsp raisins
1 tbsp garam masala
1 tsp turmeric

½ tsp cumin
½ tsp garlic powder
½ tsp onion powder
½ tsp salt
320 g vegan pastry,
    puff or shortcrust*

*Top tip: Buy ready-rolled pastry, or use a clean wine bottle as a rolling pin. See the cheap and easy pastry recipe on page 66.

METHOD

Heat the oven to 180°C, 350°F, gas mark 4. Drain the chickpeas and place them in a bowl. Give the can a rinse and put it to one side – you'll need it in a minute. Mix all the ingredients (except the pastry) in the bowl with the chickpeas.

Roll out the pastry. Use the top edge of the chickpea can to cut circles. Place a spoonful of the coronation mix into the centre of a pastry circle, place another pastry circle on top and press to seal the edges. Use a knife to create a small slit in the middle of the parcel lid and bake them for about 15 minutes.

Not keen on pastry? You can also use the filling on a jacket potato!

Veggie Curry in a Hurry

Delicious, simple and cheaper than a takeaway! Homemade curry is healthier and can be a great way to use up vegetables that are going off.

Serves 4–6

INGREDIENTS

2 cups brown rice

1 tbsp oil

2 tsp turmeric

1½ tsp garam masala

1½ tsp onion powder

1½ tsp ground cumin

1 tsp garlic powder

1 tsp salt

½ 400-g can chopped tomatoes

400-g can brown lentils

2 cups diced vegetables of your choosing

2 tbsp vegan yoghurt, or ¾ cup soy or oat milk mixed with a tsp of lemon juice

Handful of coriander, chopped (optional)

Handful of chopped almonds (optional)

METHOD

Put the rice on to boil – brown rice can take up to 30 minutes.

The key to a good curry is something called the tadka. Tadka means heating spices and aromatics to release the flavour.

Heat the oil in a pan and let it warm for a few seconds, then add all the spices and salt and use a wooden spoon to keep them moving so they don't burn.

When you start to smell the rich aromas after 1–2 minutes, add the tomatoes. Cook for 4 minutes, then add the lentils and the veg. If it's looking a bit dry, add ¼ cup of water. Simmer until the vegetables are soft, then turn the heat off and add the yoghurt or milk. Leave for a moment to warm through then serve with the rice and the coriander and almond garnish.

See pages 46–47 for pre-made tadka.

Gado-Gado to Go

Gado-gado is a popular Indonesian dish. It translates as "mix-mix" as it's a mixture of vegetables with a peanut sauce, often served as a salad. This is a simplified version.

Serves 2

INGREDIENTS

200 g tofu

1 tbsp oil

2 cups shredded cabbage

1 cup thinly sliced carrots

1 cup green beans, ends cut off

1 cup peanut butter

2 tbsp soy sauce

2 tsp sugar

3 tbsp lime or lemon juice

½ tsp dried chillies

1 cup beansprouts

½ cup sweetcorn

¼ cucumber, julienned

Handful of coriander (optional)

METHOD

Thinly slice the tofu and fry it in the oil on a medium heat until brown on both sides.

Simmer the vegetables in a medium pot of water for 5 minutes. While the vegetables are cooking, place the peanut butter, soy sauce, sugar, lime or lemon juice and dried chillies in a pan and stir over a medium heat until they are combined and warmed through.

Place the beansprouts into a bowl. Top with the warm vegetables and place the sweetcorn and cucumber on one side of the bowl. Lay the sliced tofu on top, then pour the sauce over everything and garnish with coriander.

Tricolour Pasta Punch

Pasta is a classic student dish, but can easily become dull. Spice things up with this deconstructed arrabbiata-style dish.

Serves 1

INGREDIENTS

1 cup dried penne
1 tbsp olive oil
1 red onion, thinly sliced
1 tsp chilli flakes
½ cup cherry tomatoes, halved
½ yellow pepper, diced
2 cloves garlic, crushed
1 cup baby spinach, chopped
Salt and pepper to taste

METHOD

Put the pasta on to boil.

Heat the oil in a large frying pan over a medium heat. Add the onion and fry for 3-4 minutes, then add the chilli flakes and cook for another minute.

Add the tomatoes and pepper and cook for 2-3 minutes until they're soft. Add the garlic and cook for 1 minute, then add the spinach and cook until wilted, stirring constantly.

Add the drained pasta to the frying pan. Make sure it's coated with the oil and the vegetables are stirred evenly through. Season with salt and pepper and serve immediately.

Oh My Omelette!

It turns out if you want to make an omelette, you don't need to break any eggs. Try this vegan noodle version at any time of the day to hit your protein intake.

Serves 1

INGREDIENTS

½ cup chickpea (gram) flour

½ cup plant milk

2 tbsp nutritional yeast

½ tsp turmeric

1 tsp Dijon mustard

½ tsp garlic powder

½ tsp onion powder

2 tbsp oil

1 packet ready-to-eat ramen noodles

½ cup baby spinach, chopped

Pinch of chilli flakes

1 clove garlic, crushed

Salt and pepper to taste

2 tsp soy sauce

1 spring onion, chopped

METHOD

Whisk all the "egg" ingredients - the chickpea flour, plant milk, nutritional yeast, turmeric, mustard, garlic powder and onion powder together in a bowl, using a whisk or fork.

Heat the oil in a pan until it gets warm, then stir-fry the noodles for 1-2 minutes. Add the spinach, chilli flakes, garlic and salt and pepper and fry for another minute, then add the soy sauce.

After 1 minute add the "egg" mixture, lower the heat and cook everything until the omelette is solid on one side, then flip it. Serve hot with the chopped spring onion on top.

Traffic Light Couscous

Couscous is a student staple; it's cheap, fast and filling. This delicious, rainbow recipe packs a nutritional punch too.

Serves 2

INGREDIENTS

1 sweet potato, diced
1 tbsp oil
1 cup couscous
1 cup hot stock
½ red onion, diced
1 cup kale, chopped
1 red pepper, diced
½ cup sweetcorn kernels
1 tbsp lemon juice
1 tsp mixed herbs
1 tbsp chopped fresh parsley
Salt and pepper to taste

METHOD

Heat the oven to 180°C, 350°F, gas mark 4. Coat the sweet potato in the oil, place on a greased tray and bake for 20 minutes.

Place the couscous in a bowl and add the hot stock. Stir, then cover with a lid, plate or chopping board and leave for 5-10 minutes to soak up the liquid. Use a fork to separate the grains.

Throw the onion, kale and pepper into a frying pan with a little oil and fry for 3-5 minutes. Add the vegetables and the cooked sweet potato (including the oil) to the couscous and stir. Mix in the sweetcorn kernels, lemon juice, herbs, fresh parsley and salt and pepper and serve immediately.

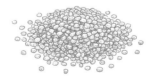

THE BATCH
IS BACK

The cheapest and most efficient way of cooking is batch cooking – cooking large quantities in one go and then freezing it. For this to work you will need a very large saucepan and freezer-safe storage pots.

The art of batch cooking is to make a large amount of a thing that is quite versatile. Some of these recipes will be a complete meal you can freeze in small portions to eat in the future, others will be a base you can use to build quick individual meals during the week.

Remember: cool food at room temperature for no more than 2 hours, never keep frozen food for more than three months, and reheat your meals using a microwave, oven or saucepan.

Batch-Baked Potatoes

Never wait for a baked potato again! Pre-bake a bunch of potatoes for easy meals later on, and just add the filling!

Makes 12

INGREDIENTS

12 baking potatoes
2 tbsp oil
1½ tsp salt

METHOD

Heat the oven to 220°C, 425°F, gas mark 7. Lightly wash the potatoes then pat them dry with a tea towel. Mix the oil and salt together in a bowl and rub the outside of each potato with the mixture so it is completely covered. Place the potatoes evenly spaced on a baking tray lined with tinfoil or greaseproof paper.

Cook them in the oven for 20 minutes, then reduce the temperature to 190°C, 375°F, gas mark 5, turn each potato, and cook for 45 minutes until the skin is crisp and the insides are soft – check with a knife. Leave them on the side, covered with a tea towel or baking paper, to cool completely.

Wrap each potato in tinfoil, store in the fridge for up to five days, or in the freezer for up to three months. Allow to defrost in the fridge overnight and reheat in the microwave for 2–4 minutes on full power. Enjoy with your favourite toppings, like the coronation curry filling from page 28, baked beans or some grated vegan cheese.

Hassle-Free Hasselback Veg

Sliced and baked root vegetables are easy to make and look beautiful on your plate. Cook at the same time as the potatoes (see pages 42–43) to save extra energy money!

Serves 4

INGREDIENTS

2 sweet potatoes
2 carrots
2 beetroots
2 parsnips
1 tbsp oil
1 tsp salt
1 whole head of garlic

METHOD

Hasselback means slicing three-quarters of the way through the vegetables, so they go soft in the middle and are crispy and delicious on the outside.

Take two chopsticks or pencils, and place them either side of the vegetable. Using a very sharp knife, cut slits in the vegetable by slicing down about ½ cm apart. When the knife hits the chopsticks/pencils you know to stop cutting.

Heat the oven to 180°C, 350°F, gas mark 4. Coat the vegetables with oil and salt and place on a greased baking tray. Peel the outer layers off the garlic, crush each clove under the flat blade of a knife, and put them in the pan with the vegetables. Roast for about 40 minutes–1 hour.

Eat immediately or allow the vegetables to cool at room temperature, then divide into four portions and freeze. Allow to defrost in the fridge overnight and reheat for a few minutes in the microwave. Serve with gravy.

Tadka Time

This is the spicy base that will give you restaurant-grade curry every time – just add the vegetables and tomatoes or coconut milk.

Serves 6

INGREDIENTS

6 tbsp oil
2 onions, minced
2 tsp turmeric
3 tsp garam masala
2 tsp salt
6 cloves garlic, minced
2 tbsp minced fresh ginger
6 tomatoes, finely diced

METHOD

Heat the oil in a frying pan over a medium heat and fry the onions gently until they are beginning to turn brown, then add the spices and salt.

Keep stirring the mixture with a wooden spoon until you smell the aromas coming through, then add the garlic and ginger and cook for about 1 minute, followed by the diced tomatoes.

Turn the heat down and allow the mixture to cook slowly. The tomatoes will reduce and it will become a thick sauce. The oil will start to separate after 5–10 minutes and at that point the tadka is done.

Allow to cool. You could add vegetables or tofu with some coconut milk to make a delicious curry. Divide into six portions and freeze.

Lentil Lovers' Bolognese

Lentils are cheap, delicious, high in protein and versatile. Serve this easy Bolognese with pasta, rice, nachos or on those pre-baked spuds!

Serves 8–10

INGREDIENTS

1 tbsp oil
1 onion, finely chopped
3 cloves garlic, minced
4 400-g cans chopped tomatoes
1 vegetable stock cube* or 1 tsp yeast extract
1 tbsp mixed herbs
4 400-g cans brown lentils
Salt and pepper to taste

*Top tip: If using a solid stock cube, grate it first to avoid clumping.

METHOD

Heat the oil in a frying pan and gently cook the chopped onion until it starts to go see-through – this will take about 5–10 minutes. Stir in the garlic, then add the tomatoes, stock and herbs.

Reduce the heat and simmer for about 30 minutes, allowing the sauce to thicken. Add the lentils and heat through for 4–5 minutes then season. Serve immediately with your choice of carbs, like a pre-baked potato, pasta, rice or in a taco. Alternatively, cool the Bolognese and freeze in portions.

If you're serving with rice or pasta, you can freeze everything in the same container for an easy-to-reheat complete meal. Just defrost overnight in the fridge and microwave for 2–3 minutes on full power.

Legendary Lasagne

Easy to bake and simple to store, this is a batch-cook winner every time.

Serves 9

INGREDIENTS

¼ cup vegan margarine

¼ cup plain flour

¼ tsp onion powder

½ tsp salt

4 cups soy or oat milk

500-g box dried lasagne sheets

½ batch of the Lentil Lovers' Bolognese on pages 48–49

METHOD

Heat the oven to 180°C, 350°F, gas mark 4. Grease a baking pan approximately 37 cm long by 24 cm wide, and 7 cm deep.

To make the white sauce, melt the margarine in a saucepan over a low heat. When it's liquid, add the flour, onion powder and salt to make a paste. Add the milk slowly while stirring continuously – you could ask a housemate to help! When finished, the sauce will be thick but pourable.

Drizzle a small layer in the bottom of the baking pan, then add a layer of lasagne sheets. Add Bolognese on top until the pan is one-third full. Drizzle another layer of white sauce then add another layer of lasagne sheets. Spread the rest of the Bolognese on top, leaving about a 1½ cm gap to the rim of the pan. Top with lasagne sheets and pour over the rest of the white sauce.

Bake for 40 minutes. Allow to cool then divide into nine squares and freeze individually. Reheat defrosted portions in the microwave on full power for 3–4 minutes.

Ultimate Irish Stew

This vegan Irish stew replaces the beef with a rich, umami tempeh and mushroom mix. A great winter treat, and just one pot to wash up!

Serves 8

INGREDIENTS

2 tbsp oil
1 large onion, diced
1 cup diced tempeh
2 cups mushrooms, sliced
4 cloves garlic, crushed
3 tbsp plain flour
330-ml can stout (optional)
5 cups vegetable stock
2 tbsp soy sauce
1 tsp salt

1 tsp ground black pepper
1 tbsp mixed herbs
1 tbsp sugar
1 bay leaf (optional)
4 potatoes, cut into 3 cm cubes
3 carrots, cut into chunks
2 parsnips, cut into chunks
3 celery sticks, diced
½ head cabbage, shredded

METHOD

Heat the oil in a large, heavy-bottomed saucepan and fry the onion for 2–3 minutes. Add the tempeh and mushrooms and fry until brown. Add the garlic and stir for 1–2 minutes, then add the flour and stir it into the oil. Add the stout if using, then the stock, soy sauce, seasoning, mixed herbs and sugar.

Bring to the boil then reduce the heat. If you're using the bay leaf, add it now. Add the potatoes and simmer for 15 minutes, then add the carrots, parsnips and celery. Simmer for another 15 minutes, then add the cabbage. Simmer for 3–5 minutes then turn off the heat.

Remove the bay leaf then divide into eight freezer-safe containers and allow to cool before freezing. When ready to use, defrost overnight in the fridge and reheat in a pan. Serve with crusty rolls.

Seitan Sandwich Slice

Seitan is the powdered gluten from flour, often called vital wheat gluten. When mixed with herbs, spices and water, it makes a delicious, high-protein meat substitute.

Serves 10–12

INGREDIENTS

2 cups vital wheat gluten
1 tbsp nutritional yeast
1 tsp celery salt
2 tsp dried mixed herbs
1 tsp smoked paprika
1 tsp cumin
1 tsp mustard powder
1 tsp salt
1 tsp ground black pepper
2½ cups vegetable stock
2 tbsp soy sauce
3 tbsp tomato paste
2 tbsp oil

METHOD

Heat the oven to 180°C, 350°F, gas mark 4. In a bowl, combine all the dry ingredients. In a jug, make up the stock and add the wet ingredients, then allow to cool. Stir continuously as you pour the liquid into the dry ingredients. The ingredients will combine quickly and become a wet dough within 2 minutes.

Turn the dough out onto a chopping board lightly sprinkled with plain flour. Knead the dough by folding it over and pressing your fists into it for 2–4 minutes. Roll the dough into a thick sausage shape and then wrap it tightly in two layers of tinfoil. Place it on a baking tray and bake for 70 minutes, then unwrap the loaf and bake for a further 15 minutes to brown the outside.

Allow to cool and refrigerate overnight. Slice into portions and freeze individually, defrosting each overnight in the fridge before use.

Top tip: Fancy a kebab? Keep this loaf whole and use a potato peeler to shave off lengths. Fry them in a pan with a little oil and serve in a pitta bread with salad.

Simple Soup

This easy pumpkin or squash soup makes a hearty, low-fat, nutritious meal or filling snack any time of the year.

Serves 6

INGREDIENTS

1 autumn pumpkin or summer squash, whole
1 tbsp olive oil
1 onion, diced
2 cloves garlic, minced
1¾ cups hot vegetable stock
Salt and pepper to taste

METHOD

Heat the oven to 200°C, 400°F, gas mark 6. Place the whole pumpkin inside the oven and bake for 40 minutes. Meanwhile, heat the oil in a pan and fry the onions until brown. Add the garlic and cook for 1 minute, then add the stock and turn off the heat.

When the pumpkin is ready, remove it from the oven and cut it open. Scoop out the seeds and stringy innards. As it cools a little you will be able to peel the skin off too. Remove the nobbles at the top and bottom then, using a fork, mash the soft pumpkin and scrape it into the pan with the stock. Stir on a low heat until it is all combined and smooth.

Divide into six portions, allow to cool and freeze. Defrost thoroughly to use, reheating it in a pan and adding salt and pepper to taste.

Genius Gazpacho

This cold soup from Spain is a delight on a hot day. This basic, no-blend version can be stored in the freezer for an easy summer lunch.

Serves 6

INGREDIENTS

10–14 tomatoes, skinned, seeded and minced
3 cloves garlic, minced
½ red onion, minced
1 green chilli, deseeded and finely diced
1 tbsp lemon juice
1 cup passata
2 tbsp olive oil
Salt and pepper to taste
½ cucumber, diced
½ green pepper, diced

METHOD

Modern gazpacho is made with a blender or a food processor, but traditionally everything was hand chopped. The key is to chop everything really finely with a very sharp knife.

Combine all the finely diced and minced ingredients and stir really well. Add the lemon juice and passata. Leave in the fridge for 2–3 hours to let the flavours combine.

Stir in the olive oil and season well, then divide into six containers. Freeze immediately and defrost overnight in the fridge. When you're ready to serve, garnish with cucumber and green pepper.

Mega Moussaka

Comforting and easy to store, this dish is perfect for a lazy mid-week meal.

Serves 9

INGREDIENTS

1 aubergine, cut into 1-cm-thick slices

Pinch of salt

4 potatoes, boiled and mashed

½ batch of the Lentil Lovers' Bolognese on pages 48–49

1 batch of the white sauce from the Legendary Lasagne on page 50

METHOD

Heat the oven to 200°C, 400°F, gas mark 6. Lay the aubergine slices out on a greased baking tray and sprinkle with salt. Roast for 10 minutes in the oven. Grease the lasagne dish. Place a layer of mashed potato on the bottom, then layer the aubergine slices on top. Add the Bolognese on top of that, and finally pour the white sauce over to finish. Bake for 20 minutes in the oven.

Overnight Oats

Tasty and cost effective, overnight oats are perfect all year round. Freeze as is and add your toppings later to enjoy.

Serves 6

INGREDIENTS

1½ tsp ground
   cinnamon

3 cups porridge oats

3 cups soy or oat milk

Pinch of salt

METHOD

Place all the ingredients in a bowl and stir to combine, then leave overnight in the fridge to soak. In the morning, divide six portions into freezable containers. You can freeze overnight oats for up to six months and defrost them overnight in the fridge. Just add your toppings when you're ready to eat. You could try summer fruits and yoghurt; grated carrots, crushed walnuts and maple syrup; sliced banana and peanut butter or a big spoonful of jam!

Multipurpose Muffins

This can be eaten as a quick, cold snack or reheated to be the main event alongside those hasselback vegetables from pages 44–45.

Serves 6–8

INGREDIENTS

1 onion, diced
2 tbsp oil
1 tbsp nutritional yeast
2 tsp ground linseed
2 tsp yeast extract in ¾ cup hot water
1¼ cups chopped nuts
2 tbsp ground almonds
1 carrot, grated
2 slices toast, grated into crumbs
1 tbsp mixed herbs
Salt and pepper to taste

METHOD

Heat the oven to 180°C, 350°F, gas mark 4. Fry the onion in the oil until brown, then add it into a bowl with all the other ingredients and mix everything together.

Grease a muffin tray (or place muffin cups on a baking tray) and fill the cups with a generous helping of the mixture - this should make about eight muffins. Bake for 20 minutes.

Allow to cool and freeze individually. Reheat in the microwave once defrosted for 2–3 minutes on full power.

Craveable Tomato Cornbread

Popular in America, cornbread is often served with syrup. This sundried tomato version makes a delicious savoury breakfast to have on the go.

Serves 10

INGREDIENTS

2 tsp apple cider vinegar
1½ cups soy or oat milk
1½ cups cornmeal
¾ cup plain flour
1 tbsp baking powder
½ tsp salt
¼ cup melted vegan butter
¼ cup oil
1 tbsp mixed herbs
½ cup chopped sundried tomatoes

METHOD

Heat the oven to 200°C, 400°F, gas mark 6. Mix the vinegar and milk together and put aside to curdle (this is when the mixture separates into two distinct parts – usually lumps and liquid). Combine the cornmeal, flour, baking powder and salt in a bowl. Make a hole in the middle and add all the wet ingredients, mixing with a whisk or fork until the mixture is smooth like batter.

Add the herbs and the sundried tomatoes, and then pour the mixture into a greased lasagne dish. Bake in the oven for 25–30 minutes, until golden brown. Allow to cool and then freeze in portions.

Perfect Pastry

A stock of pastry can help you use up leftovers, make a quick snack, or whip up an individual pie for lunch.

Makes enough for three large pies, ten pasties or 30 cheese straws

INGREDIENTS

1½ cups vegan butter block
6 cups plain flour
6 tsp cold water

METHOD

Cut the butter into cubes and place them in a bowl, then add the flour. Using clean fingers, rub the flour and butter together until the mixture looks like breadcrumbs. Add the cold water and use your hands to squeeze it together to form a dough.

If it's a bit crumbly, add another teaspoon of water. Tip it on to a lightly floured, clean work surface and roll into a smooth and springy dough. Chill for 20 minutes before use, or cut into portions and freeze. Defrost in the fridge overnight and then use to make pies, pasties, cheese straws or tarts!

Top tip: Choose a vegan butter block that's high in fat (rather than margarine, which is high in water) for the best results.

COMFORT FOOD

Sometimes you just need to feel good. And sometimes feeling good means eating good. The next few pages are dedicated to recipes that will perk you up when you're feeling down. Because while student life can be fun, busy and exciting, it can also be intense. Feeling a bit homesick? Didn't do quite so well in that assignment? Got a touch of freshers' flu? We've got the feel-good food for you.

You don't need to feel bad to want to eat something that'll make you feel good. Among the cosy and comforting recipes in this book, we've also included party food, picnic treats and sharing plates so you can feed your hungry friends. Food, after all, is almost always better when it's shared.

Fantastic Fry-Up

There's nothing more comforting than a cooked breakfast. This dish is a healthy alternative to the traditional greasy-spoon option.

Serves 1

INGREDIENTS

1 potato
½ tsp smoked paprika
½ tsp tomato paste
1 tsp soy sauce
½ tsp sugar
Salt and pepper to taste
2 thin slices tempeh
1 medium tomato
1 portobello mushroom
1 tbsp lemon juice
1 tbsp oil
Handful of spinach

METHOD

Heat the oven to 180°C, 350°F, gas mark 4. Cut the potato in half and place it in a saucepan of boiling water for 5 minutes. Mix the paprika, tomato paste, soy sauce, sugar, and salt and pepper in a bowl. Place the tempeh slices in the bowl so the marinade covers them completely.

Cut the tomato in half and place on a lightly greased baking tray with the mushroom. Cover them in the lemon juice and season with salt and pepper.

Remove the potato from the water and slice in ½-cm coins. Lay the coins on the baking tray next to the tomato and mushroom and season with salt. Bake for 30 minutes.

Heat the oil in a pan and fry the tempeh "bacon" for 4 minutes on each side. Add the remainder of the marinade to the pan and fry for another minute. Blanch the spinach in boiling water for up to 30 seconds. Drain using a sieve or colander, and press the spinach with the back of a fork to remove excess water. Place the spinach on a plate and lay the "bacon" on top. Add the potato, tomato and mushroom and, if you'd like, serve with a decent spoonful of tomato sauce!

Posh American-Style Pancakes

This super simple pancake recipe is great for a leisurely brunch or as the base of an evening meal.

Serves 4–6

INGREDIENTS

1¾ cups and 2 tbsp self-raising flour
Pinch of salt
1 tsp baking powder
1¾ cups soy or oat milk
2 tbsp vegetable oil

METHOD

Add the flour, salt and baking powder to the bowl and stir so they're evenly mixed. Add the milk and use a whisk to combine everything so the mixture is thick and doesn't have any lumps.

Let the mixture stand for 15 minutes, then start to heat ½ tbsp oil in the pan. Swirl it so it coats the base of the pan.

When the oil is hot, add a scant cup of pancake mixture to the pan. It should spread out slowly. Reduce the heat to medium-low and let the pancake cook until all the bubbles on the surface have popped. Then flip the pancake over using a flat spatula. Cook on the other side for 1 minute.

Serve with lemon and sugar, bananas, syrup and tempeh "bacon", or with the Bolognese (see pages 48-49).

Shakshuka Sunday

Traditionally made with eggs, this tofu version is an easy alternative for a delicious weekend brunch.

Serves 4

INGREDIENTS

2 tbsp olive oil

1 onion, chopped

1 green pepper, deseeded and cut into chunks

1 red pepper, deseeded and cut into chunks

1 orange pepper, deseeded and cut into chunks

2 garlic cloves, finely chopped

1 tsp ground cumin

1 tsp ground coriander

1 tsp smoked paprika

Pinch of cayenne pepper (optional)

2 400-g cans chopped tomatoes

2 batches of the Tofu Scramble on page 76

2 tbsp chopped fresh coriander

METHOD

Pour the oil into a large frying pan over a medium heat. Fry the onion, peppers and garlic for 6-8 minutes or until soft.

Add the spices and cook for a further 1-2 minutes, stirring constantly. Mix in the tomatoes and simmer for 5-10 minutes to reduce and thicken the sauce.

Make four wells in the sauce and heap in the tofu. Cook for a further 5 minutes, sprinkle the coriander over the top then serve hot with crusty bread.

Tofu Scramble

A delicious egg alternative that can be served on toast, in a sandwich or as an accompaniment to a variety of other dishes, including the shakshuka on page 74.

Serves 2

INGREDIENTS

350 g firm tofu, drained

½ tsp kala namak (black salt) or salt

2 tbsp nutritional yeast

1 tsp onion powder

2 tsp turmeric

1 tsp ground cumin

2 tbsp oil

METHOD

Crumble the tofu into a bowl and add the salt, yeast and spices. Mix everything together. Heat the oil in a pan, add the tofu mixture and fry on a medium heat for 5-10 minutes. Add a little water if the mixture gets dry. Serve immediately or allow to cool and mix with vegan mayonnaise and chives for a sandwich.

Toasty Tomatoes

This baked tomatoes-on-toast recipe makes for perfect comfort food.

Serves 4

INGREDIENTS

2 cups cherry
   tomatoes
1 tsp balsamic vinegar
2 tbsp olive oil
2 garlic cloves, minced

1 tsp mixed herbs
½ tsp salt
1 tsp pepper
4 slices toast

METHOD

Heat the oven to 200°C, 400°F, gas mark 6. Combine all the ingredients in a bowl and mix, making sure the tomatoes are covered. Pour the tomatoes into a greased baking dish and bake for 15–20 minutes. Serve directly on to the toast. Top tip: Use hummus instead of butter on the toast and add a little rocket for a delicious lunch!

Mid-Week Mac

An easy and comforting one-pot meal perfect for any night of the week.

Serves 4

INGREDIENTS

1½ cups dried macaroni
2 tbsp vegan margarine
1 tsp Dijon mustard
2 tbsp nutritional yeast
1 tsp garlic powder
1 tsp onion powder
½ tsp salt
2 tbsp flour
¾ cup soy or oat milk
1 cup frozen sweetcorn kernels
1 cup halved cherry tomatoes

METHOD

Fill a medium saucepan with water and bring to the boil. Add the macaroni and cook according to the instructions on the packet. Take it off the heat 1 minute ahead of schedule and strain, so that the pasta will be very firm, then put the pasta to one side.

In the saucepan, add the margarine, mustard and dry ingredients except the flour. Heat so the margarine melts, then add the flour and mix into a paste. Stir in the milk slowly (so there are no lumps) and simmer gently for 5 minutes, then add the pasta. Keep simmering until the sauce is thick. Take off the heat and add the sweetcorn and tomatoes. Serve immediately.

Banging Bhajis

Whether it's a movie night or a study night, a stack of bhajis will bring everyone together.

Makes 24

INGREDIENTS

Oil, for deep frying
2 cups chickpea (gram) flour
1 tsp baking powder
1 tsp turmeric
1 tsp cumin
1 tsp fennel seeds (optional)
½ tsp chilli powder
½ tsp salt
⅔ cup water
4 onions, thinly sliced

METHOD

Fill half a small saucepan or wok with oil and heat for about 5 minutes over a medium heat.

In a bowl, stir together the dry ingredients making sure the spices are fully incorporated. Pour in the water and mix until you have a stiff paste. Add the onions and stir until they're completely covered by the wet mix.

Get a small spot of batter on a teaspoon and drop it into the oil. If the oil is hot enough the batter will start to bubble immediately. If not, wait 2 minutes then test again.

Use a tablespoon to scoop a measure of the mix and use a second spoon to scrape it off into the hot oil. Fry the mixture for 3-4 minutes until golden brown and crispy. Carefully scoop the bhajis out of the oil and place them on kitchen roll to drain. Serve with mango chutney.

Wild-Grown Wings

If you think you don't like cauliflower, think again. These buffalo wing-style cauliflower pieces are mind-blowingly good.

Serves 4

INGREDIENTS

¾ cup plain flour

1 tsp paprika

2 tsp garlic powder

1 tsp salt

½ tsp pepper

¾ cup soy or oat milk

1 cauliflower head

¼ cup hot sauce

2 tbsp coconut oil

1 tbsp golden syrup

METHOD

Heat the oven to 230°C, 450°F, gas mark 8. Grease a baking tray. In a large bowl, add the flour, paprika, garlic powder, salt, pepper and milk and mix well.

Cut the cauliflower up into individual flowering stems, called florets. Drop them into the mixture and make sure the cauliflower is well coated. Using tongs or two forks, remove the florets and place them on the baking tray. Bake for 10 minutes, then turn them over and bake for another 10 minutes.

In a separate bowl, mix the hot sauce, coconut oil and golden syrup together. Remove the cauliflower and coat with the hot sauce mix, then return to the oven and bake for another 20 minutes. Serve as a snack with dips, use in tacos or as a pizza topping.

Nachos Now

You've finished that essay with half an hour to spare before that gig, sports game or society social you've been looking forward to. Smash out this speedy meal with time for a shower!

Serves 1

INGREDIENTS

200-g can baked beans
1 cup plain tortilla chips
¼ cup grated vegan cheese (optional)
1 tomato
¼ red onion
½ tsp olive oil
¼ tsp paprika
Squeeze of lemon
Salt and pepper to taste
1 tbsp vegan yoghurt

METHOD

Empty the beans into a saucepan and place on a low heat on the hob. Don't let the beans boil.

While they are heating, place the tortilla chips on a baking tray and sprinkle over the grated cheese. Place the cheesy tortilla chips under a grill for a few minutes to brown. Skip this step if you're not using the cheese.

Finely dice the tomato and onion, place them into a bowl with the olive oil, paprika and lemon and mix. Add salt and pepper to taste.

Take the beans off the hob. Transfer the chips to a plate, pour the beans over the top, and serve with the tomato mix and the yoghurt.

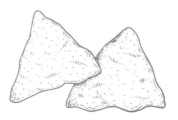

Sweet Potato Juggernauts

These high-fibre, complex-carb dream boats will be an immovable nutritional force – keeping you dancing, working out or studying through the night.

Serves 1

INGREDIENTS

1 sweet potato
½ 400-g can chickpeas
1 tsp oil
½ tsp cumin
½ tsp coriander
½ tsp cinnamon
½ tsp paprika
1 tbsp hummus
1 tsp lemon juice
½ tsp mixed herbs
1 garlic clove, crushed

METHOD

Heat the oven to 180°C, 350°F, gas mark 4. Use a fork to pierce the skin of the sweet potato, then pop it in the microwave on full power for 5 minutes, turning it halfway through the cooking time.

Drain the chickpeas and mix them with the oil, cumin, coriander, cinnamon and paprika. Place them on a greased tray and bake for 10–15 minutes.

Add the hummus, lemon juice, mixed herbs and garlic into a bowl and stir. Add a little water to thin it into a sauce.

Cut the sweet potato in half and use a spoon to scoop out a bit of the flesh. Mix it with the chickpeas then load it back into the skins. Pour the sauce over the top and serve.

Syrup Sponge Turnover

A delicious dessert you can make in minutes and share with friends, this syrup sponge ticks all the sweet-tooth boxes.

Serves 4

INGREDIENTS

½ cup soy milk
1 tsp lemon juice
¼ cup caster sugar
¼ cup vegan butter
¾ cup self-raising flour
½ tsp salt
½ tsp baking powder
4 tbsp golden syrup
1 banana, sliced

METHOD

Pour the soy milk into a small bowl and add the lemon juice. Leave for 5 minutes to curdle.

In another bowl, mix together the sugar and butter using a whisk or fork. You're trying to cream it, or fully combine it so it looks pale with air pockets. Add the flour, salt and baking powder and mix until stiff. Add the curdled milk and stir together.

Pour the golden syrup into the base of a lightly greased microwave-proof bowl. Then add the cake mixture on top. Cook in the microwave for 3 minutes. If you give it a wobble the sponge will seem "set", like a jelly.

Allow it to cool for a couple of minutes then place a plate on top and turn it over to reveal the syrup-topped pudding underneath. Layer the sliced banana over the top and serve.

BIG BRAIN ENERGY

Sometimes you just need a snack to get you through. Here's a mix of easy-to-make snacks and sweet treats that are great brain fuel, packed full of good stuff and are totally moreish with no preservatives or dodgy colourings.

Some can be made quickly to satisfy a craving, others need a bit of prep but can be stored. Some are for sharing and others are just for one. Whether it's midnight munchies when you get home from a night out, or mid-essay energy when that deadline is looming, these snacks offer a balance between good nutrition and satisfying that craving!

The Ultimate Vegan Sandwich

Nothing beats food to go like a well-made sandwich. You'll be making this incredible tempeh toastie time and time again!

Serves 1

INGREDIENTS

½ **avocado**

Pinch of salt

1 **tbsp lemon juice**

2 **slices wholegrain bread**

4 **sundried tomatoes, chopped**

Handful of rocket

4 **slices tempeh**

1 **tbsp oil**

2 **tbsp white wine vinegar**

2 **tbsp soy sauce**

½ **tbsp sugar**

METHOD

Using the back of a fork, mash the avocado with the salt and lemon juice until it's a paste. Spread it over one slice of the bread. Place the sundried tomatoes and rocket on top.

In a pan, fry the tempeh in the oil for a couple of minutes each side to brown. Then add the vinegar, soy sauce and sugar. Reduce the heat and keep it moving in the pan so it doesn't burn.

When the sauce has become very sticky, remove the tempeh and lay across the dressed slice of bread. Add the lid of the sandwich and slice down the middle. Voilà!

Creamy Cucumber Pittas

This is a super lunchtime recipe, easy and cheap to make and keeps in the fridge for three days. It also works as a tasty side dish!

Serves 2

INGREDIENTS

1 cucumber, thinly sliced

½ white onion, thinly sliced

⅔ cup vegan yoghurt

2 tbsp lemon juice

½ tsp salt

Pepper to taste

½ cup chopped green olives (optional)

2 pitta breads

METHOD

Combine the cucumber, onion and yoghurt together in a bowl, then add the lemon juice, salt and pepper. Lightly toast the pitta breads and fill them with the cucumber mixture and green olives if you're using them.

Lazy Lentil Dip

This luscious lentil appetizer takes 15 minutes from start to finish. Serve warm with pitta breads and carrot sticks, or cool in the fridge and use as a sandwich filling.

Serves 2

INGREDIENTS

½ cup dried red lentils, rinsed

1 cup water

½ tbsp olive oil

1 garlic clove, peeled and crushed or minced

½ tsp paprika

½ tsp ground cumin

½ tsp salt

METHOD

Place the lentils and water in a saucepan and bring to the boil. Simmer until the lentils are soft, for around 10 minutes. Take them off the heat, drain any excess water, then add the rest of the ingredients and stir. Mash any whole lentils with the back of a fork. Serve warm with pitta bread, toast or vegetable sticks.

Ants on a Log

A high-protein family classic!

Serves 1

INGREDIENTS

1 stick celery
2 tsp peanut butter
12 raisins

METHOD

Top and tail the celery stick then cut it into four small sections. Spread the peanut butter into the groove of the celery and space the raisins out along the "log". Variations include almonds, blueberries or chocolate chips as the "ants". Don't like celery? Try using a halved banana as the "log".

Apple Ahoy!

These crunchy apple boats are sweet, savoury and super satisfying.

Serves 1

INGREDIENTS

1 tbsp vegan cream cheese or hummus
1 apple, cored and sliced in two
1 tsp sweet chilli sauce

METHOD

Pour the vegan cream cheese or hummus into the well of the apple where the core used to be. Drizzle the sweet chilli sauce on top. Yo-ho-ho!

Chilli Chickpeas

These spicy snacks are a healthy and delicious alternative to crisps.

Serves 4

INGREDIENTS

400-g can chickpeas
1 tsp oil
1 tbsp garam masala
½ tsp ground chilli
½ tsp salt

METHOD

Heat the oven to 200°C, 400°F, gas mark 6. Put all the ingredients into a plastic container with a lid and shake until the chickpeas are well coated and the spices have been mixed through. Pour the chickpeas onto a greased baking tray and bake for 30 minutes, stirring halfway. Leave them to cool for the ultimate crunch.

Perfect Popcorn

Popcorn is the ultimate movie-night snack! It's also light, healthy and affordable to make yourself.

Serves 4

INGREDIENTS

⅓ cup popcorn kernels
½ tsp salt

METHOD

Place a non-stick pan with a lid on the hob and heat for 2 minutes. If the pan doesn't have a lid, cover it with a heat-proof chopping board. Add the popcorn kernels, cover the pan and lower the heat slightly. Keeping the pan on the heat, gently swirl it to keep the kernels moving so they don't burn. After 1 minute you should start to hear the popping. Keep swirling until the popping slows down to every 2–3 seconds, then take off the heat, add salt and enjoy!

Brain Balls

Whip up a batch of these as an easy study snack. Keep hunger at bay and the neurons firing!

Makes 50

INGREDIENTS

2 cups peanut butter

½ cup golden syrup, or maple or agave

1 tsp vanilla extract

½ cup rolled oats

½ cup ground flaxseed

½ tsp salt

½ cup raisins or dried apple cubes

METHOD

Combine the peanut butter, golden syrup and vanilla extract together in a bowl using a wooden spoon. Add the oats, flaxseed and salt and mix slowly. When the mixture is too stiff to stir, use your clean hands to combine the raisins or apple and then start rolling heaped tablespoons of batter into balls. Place them in the fridge to firm up a little. They keep for up to five days or you can freeze them.

Mega Mug Cake

Want a quick hit of something sweet? This is the recipe for you.

Serves 1

INGREDIENTS

2 tbsp plain flour

2 tbsp cocoa powder (or vegan hot chocolate powder)

2 tbsp granulated sugar

¼ tsp baking powder

½ tsp ground linseed

1 tbsp vegetable oil

3 tbsp soy or oat milk (if using hot chocolate powder, replace one spoon with water)

1 tbsp chocolate chips

METHOD

Stir together the dry ingredients in a large microwaveable mug. Add the wet ingredients and combine well using a fork. Sprinkle the chocolate chips over the top and microwave on full power for 50–60 seconds. Let it stand for 30 seconds before tucking in!

Cookie Time

Make up a batch of these delicious cookies, perfect for dunking in hot chocolate or packing for a picnic.

Makes 24

INGREDIENTS

1 cup vegan margarine
1 cup caster sugar
4 tbsp soy or oat milk
1 tsp vanilla extract
2 ½ cups plain flour
2 tsp baking powder
Pinch of salt
2 cups chocolate chips

METHOD

Heat the oven to 180°C, 350°F, gas mark 4. Beat the margarine and sugar together with an electric hand whisk or wooden spoon until combined. Add the milk and vanilla extract, and then add the flour, baking powder and salt – if you can sift it in with a sieve you will get a better result.

Add the chocolate chips and stir them in evenly. Divide into 24 small balls and place them on a greased baking tray leaving space for them to expand. Use the back of a fork to squish the cookies slightly before baking.

Cook for 18–20 minutes. Leave to cool on the tray for 5 minutes then transfer to a wire rack or a cold plate and leave to cool completely.

GOURMET DAY

Every gourmet has their day, and student life often calls for an affordable but creative celebration meal. Whether it's a birthday, date, family visit or results day, these dishes will knock the socks off your mates who really didn't know there was a secret top chef hiding behind your studies.

Fancy food doesn't have to be tricky, and often the simplest flavours served well are the best. These recipes will help you create restaurant-style signature dishes that combine fresh flavours for a brilliant, budget feast.

Couple any special meal with a tablecloth and napkins, a candle and gentle background music for effect. Part-baked rolls from the supermarket are easy to serve as a warm side, or why not collect some wildflowers as a table arrangement?

Cool as a Cucumber

These cucumber blinis are so simple, yet they make an unusual and satisfying starter to any meal.

Serves 4

INGREDIENTS

1 cucumber
1 cup vegan yoghurt
1 garlic clove, minced
1 tbsp fresh dill
½ tbsp olive oil

½ tbsp lemon juice
¾ cup green or black olives, halved
Salt and pepper to taste

METHOD

Cut off a quarter of the cucumber and grate it into a sieve. Leave it to stand for 10 minutes so the excess moisture can drain. Mix the cucumber with the rest of the ingredients (except the olives) in a bowl and season. Chill in the fridge for an hour. Slice the remainder of the cucumber into coins and arrange on a plate. Add a spoonful of the mixture to each coin, then dress with half an olive, season and serve.

Tadka Dal

A familiar restaurant classic across the globe, dress it up for an evening meal that is so delicious your dinner guests will need to see the washing up to believe it wasn't a takeaway.

Serves 4

INGREDIENTS

1 batch of the tadka on pages 46–47
1½ cups yellow split peas, cooked
2 cups water
Handful of coriander
Salt and pepper to taste

METHOD

Heat the tadka gently in a pan, then add the split peas and water. Bring to the boil then simmer for 30 minutes until reduced into a thick sauce. Chop the coriander and add two-thirds of it to the tadka and stir in. Season, then serve in a bowl with the rest of the coriander on top. Top tip: Garnish with the Chilli Chickpeas from page 98.

Mushroom Penne

This straightforward recipe makes a really impressive meal for a special occasion, and it's also deceptively cheap!

Serves 4

INGREDIENTS

4 cups dried penne pasta
Pinch of salt
1 onion
1 tbsp olive oil
4 cups mushrooms
2 garlic cloves, finely chopped or crushed
1 tsp dried mixed herbs
4 tbsp flour
1¾ cups soy or oat milk
½ vegetable stock cube
Salt and pepper to taste
1 tsp Dijon mustard

METHOD

Fill the saucepan with boiling water from the kettle, add the pasta and a pinch of salt, and set it to simmer for 10–12 minutes.

Chop the onion and place it in the frying pan with the olive oil over a low heat. Allow the onion to cook gently, going see-through without browning. Meanwhile, slice the mushrooms. Add them to the onions and allow them to cook down for about 10 minutes; they will add water to the pan. Add the garlic and mixed herbs, stir them in, and leave it for about 1 minute.

Add the flour to the pan and coat the mushrooms. Then add the milk slowly while stirring. Once all the milk is added, crumble the stock cube into the mixture along with the salt, pepper and mustard and allow it to simmer for 2–3 minutes. Combine the sauce with the pasta and serve.

Smokey Spanish Stew

This is a job for the hob, and once prepared it can simmer in the background giving you a chance to socialize until you're ready to eat.

Serves 4

INGREDIENTS

1 onion, chopped
1 tbsp oil
2 cloves garlic, minced
½ tsp salt
1 tsp paprika
1 tsp cumin
3 400-g cans chopped tomatoes
400-g can chickpeas
2 cups baby spinach, chopped
½ cup green olives, pitted and in brine (optional)
Pepper and Tabasco to taste

METHOD

Caramelize the chopped onion in the oil on a low heat. This should take 5-10 minutes. Add the garlic, salt and spices and fry on a slightly higher heat for a further 1-2 minutes.

Add the chopped tomatoes, lower the heat and allow to reduce to a thick sauce over the course of about 1 hour. Add the chickpeas and the chopped spinach and cook for a further 5 minutes until the spinach is fully wilted. Add the olives if using, and season with pepper and Tabasco. Serve warm with crusty bread.

Katsu Comfort

Katsu curry is a nutritional delight that is easy to make, yet looks very impressive on the plate.

Serves 4–6

INGREDIENTS

2 cups brown rice

2 slices toast

¾ cup and 1 tsp cornflour

½ cup plain flour

½ cup water

Pinch of salt

1 cup and 2 tbsp oil

1 squash or small pumpkin, sliced into 1-cm wide wedges

2 tbsp mild curry powder

2 tsp onion powder

1½ tsp garlic powder

1 tsp ground ginger

1 tsp turmeric

1¾ cups vegetable stock

1 tsp lemon juice

1 tsp soy sauce

1 tsp sugar

METHOD

Put the rice on to boil first, then heat the oven to 150°C, 300°F, gas mark 2.

Coarsely grate the toast into a bowl to make breadcrumbs. In another bowl, mix ¾ cup cornflour, the flour, water and salt. Pour 1 cup of oil into a small pan and heat until bubbling. It should be deep enough to cover half the squash. Take the spears of squash and coat them in the flour mix, then roll them in the breadcrumbs to make the "katsu". Place them in the oil and allow them to cook for up to 5 minutes each side. Put them on a baking tray and place in the oven for a further 10–15 minutes until the squash is soft all the way through.

To make the sauce, heat 2 tbsp oil, add the spices and season with salt. Cook over a medium heat for a few minutes until you smell the aromatics coming through. Add the vegetable stock and leave to simmer.

In a separate dish, combine 1 tsp cornflour with the lemon juice, soy sauce and sugar and stir into a paste. Add it to the sauce and stir it in. Simmer the sauce and allow it to thicken. Place the "katsu" on a bed of rice, then drizzle the sauce over and serve.

Tarte Tatin

An easy, yet visually impressive dessert best served with vanilla ice cream.

Serves 4–6

INGREDIENTS

½ cup caster sugar
6 apples
2 thyme sprigs
⅓ cup vegan butter block
300 g vegan puff pastry

METHOD

Heat the oven to 180°C, 350°F, gas mark 4. Take a shallow sided ovenproof dish, ideally a 23 cm round tart tin, and grease it. Coat the bottom evenly with the sugar and place in the oven. You are waiting for the sugar to caramelize; this could take about 10 minutes.

Peel and core the apples and cut them into quarters. Remove the caramelized sugar from the oven and arrange the apples and thyme in the base of the pan on their sides. Try and make a pattern but keep them tightly packed.

Melt the butter and pour it over the top of the apples. Place them back in the oven and bake for about 20 minutes. Remove the dish and lay the pastry over the top of the apples, tucking the edges down the sides. Bake for 30 minutes and let stand for a further 5 minutes. Then run a knife around the edge, place a chopping board over the top of the dish and flip it so the tart is now sitting on the board apple-side up.

HAPPY HOUR

No student can survive on water (and alcohol) alone! Well, you can, but student life is a lot more colourful than that! In this chapter you will discover delicious drink recipes that can be served alongside a meal. They are low in sugar and packed full of essential vitamins and minerals to help you study, play sport and socialize with your friends.

Staying hydrated is essential to good mental and physical health, keeping you alert and focused, and helping you to sleep at night. You can also pack a lot of nutrition into a glass of liquid, topping up your healthy food choices.

These drinks are easy to make in batches or as a one-off to start your day, wrap up your evening or enjoy with friends.

Shake That Thang

This no-blender smoothie makes a great breakfast, a wholesome snack or a healthy dessert.

Serves 1

INGREDIENTS

½ cup vegan yoghurt

½ cup water

1 tbsp maple syrup

½ tsp vanilla extract

1 very ripe banana, thoroughly mashed

1 tbsp peanut butter (optional)

2 tsp cocoa powder (optional)

METHOD

Add the yoghurt, water, maple syrup and vanilla extract to a container with a lid. Shake vigorously until all mixed together. Put the mashed banana in the bottom of a glass, add the shaken smoothie mix and stir until combined. Mix the banana with peanut butter or cocoa powder before adding the liquid to try different flavours. Serve over ice.

Lemon Kicker

Traditional lemonade is a classic sunshine drink. Enjoy it the old-fashioned way or add a modern kick.

Serves 6

INGREDIENTS

2 unwaxed lemons or
1 cup pre-squeezed
lemon juice

1 cup caster sugar

1 cup warm water

3–4 cups iced water

3 slices fresh ginger
(optional)

2 sprigs rosemary
(optional)

METHOD

If using real lemons, grate the skin (zest) finely and collect it in a bowl. Cut the lemons in half and squeeze them over a hand juicer, or use a fork to pierce the flesh and squeeze them to extract the juice. Mix the juice, caster sugar and warm water together, allowing the sugar to dissolve. Pour this into a glass then top up with iced water. If you'd like, add ginger or rosemary to the syrup and chill for 30 minutes.

Spill the Tea

It's easy to forget to buy fruit juice at the shops, but if you've got tea bags then this refreshing iced tea is simple to make and keeps for two weeks.

Serves 6

INGREDIENTS

8 cups water
6 teabags

⅓ cup maple syrup or
   sugar
2 slices lemon

METHOD

Place 4 cups of water in a saucepan and bring to the boil. Take off the heat and add the teabags and the syrup or sugar. Allow the teabags to soak (also called "to steep") for up to 10 minutes. If you prefer a milder flavour, take them out earlier. Remove the teabags and allow the tea to cool. Then pour into a jug with the slices of lemon and top up with the remaining water. Keep in the fridge so it's nice and cool.

Catching Zs

Try this warming bedtime drink to help you sleep.

Serves 2

INGREDIENTS

1 tbsp coconut oil

1 thumb tip-sized
piece of fresh ginger,
grated

1½ tsp ground turmeric

½ tsp ground cinnamon

½ cup soy or oat milk

1 tbsp almond butter

½ tsp vanilla extract

1 tbsp maple syrup

Boiling water

Pinch of freshly
ground pepper

METHOD

Warm the coconut oil over a medium heat and add the ginger, turmeric and cinnamon. Add the milk, almond butter, vanilla extract and maple syrup and bring to a simmer. When the milk is heated through and the ingredients are well mixed, take off the heat and divide between two cups. Top up with boiling water and sprinkle the black pepper over the top.

Conclusion

Well, you made it to the end of the book, but not the end of your culinary journey! If you've mastered even ten of these recipes you'll have a great repertoire to see you through your studies and into adult life. Keep practising the rest and remember, if it goes wrong, that's part of the fun! Turn that gloopy curry into tomorrow's soup. Re-fry those potatoes for breakfast. Wrap that lentil Bolognese in pastry and bake it. There's almost always a save, so try not to freak out – it will be fine.

Remember as well, recipes aren't meant to stay the same. These recipes are a gift for you to follow at first, and then to make them your own. Now is the time to experiment, so if you didn't quite like something, or thought it needed less sugar, more salt or a pinch of chilli powder, give it a go! Keep a pen in the kitchen and scribble your notes in the margins. Buy yourself a notebook to write down your own versions of these recipes – and one day you will be creating new dishes from scratch.

Hopefully this book has pulled you out of a culinary wilderness and into a forest full of food and friendship. Now that you are armed and ready to explore the world of cruelty-free cooking, may it bring you joy.

Resources

BOOKS

Karolina Tegelaar, *The Vegan Baking Bible* (2022)

Kimberley Wilson, *Unprocessed: How the Food We Eat Is Fuelling Our Mental Health Crisis* (2023)

Nik Sharma, *The Flavour Equation: The Science of Great Cooking Explained* (2020)

Niki Segnit, *The Flavour Thesaurus: More Flavours: Plant-led Pairings, Recipes and Ideas for Cooks* (2023)

Richard Makin, *Anything You Can Cook, I Can Cook Vegan* (2023)

BLOGS

Forks Over Knives – www.forksoverknives.com

It Doesn't Taste Like Chicken – www.itdoesnttastelikechicken.com

Lazy Cat Kitchen – www.lazycatkitchen.com

The Minimalist Vegan – www.theminimalistvegan.com

Your Daily Vegan – www.yourdailyvegan.com

PODCASTS

Brown Vegan

Plant-Based Health Professionals

The Veganuary Podcast

WEBSITES

Bosh – www.bosh.tv

Cheap Lazy Vegan – www.youtube.com/c/CheapLazyVegan

Gaz Oakley Chef – www.gazoakleychef.com

THE LITTLE BOOK OF PASTA

Rufus Cavendish

Paperback

978-1-80007-841-3

Whether fresh, dried, baked into lasagna or swirled as spaghetti around your fork, pasta is fantastic. From farfalle and fusilli to fettucine and beyond, this pocket guide serves up a celebration of one of the world's most popular foods. With history, trivia, tips and recipes, it's got all the information and inspiration you could hunger for.

**THE LITTLE
BOOK OF
CHILLIES**

Rufus Cavendish

Paperback

978-1-80007-416-3

This book is a celebration of the all-conquering capsicum
– from mild varieties to red-hot peppers – served with a
spicy side of trivia, tips and recipes. The perfect pocket
guide to these wonders of nature, it explores how they
became so widely loved, where their heat comes from,
and how they can beguile and benefit our bodies.

Have you enjoyed this book?
If so, find us on Facebook at
SUMMERSDALE PUBLISHERS, on Twitter/X at
@SUMMERSDALE and on Instagram and TikTok at
@SUMMERSDALEBOOKS and get in touch.
We'd love to hear from you!

WWW.SUMMERSDALE.COM